AEC

& ANGISTRI

today

ΕΚΔΟΣΕΙΣ
ΤΕΧΝΗ
EDITIONS

© Copyright 2004   MICHAEL TOUBIS PUBLICATIONS S.A.
Nisiza Karela, Koropi, Attiki.
Telephone: +30 210 6029974, Fax: +30 210 6646856
Web Site: http://www.toubis.gr

ISBN: 960-540-461-3

Detail from the temple of Apha

Next page: The town of Aegi

CONTENTS

The islands of the Argolic and Saronic Gulfs are priceless jewels, gracing both gulfs with their bountiful beauty.

The Athenians are lucky that they can reach these islands in such a short time, far from the nosy city..

Three of the five largest islands of the Argosaronic – Salamis, Aegina and Poros – are located within the Saronic Gulf, the gulf between the coasts of Attica and the Peloponnese.

There is a rich ancient Greek mythology relating to these islands, and the mythology of the gulf that surrounds them is just as abundant.

It is said that it took its name from Saron, the King of ancient Troezen in the Peloponnese, opposite Poros. Once when hunting a deer, Saron fell into the sea and drowned. From then on the gulf was named the Saronic.

Hydra, along with the island of Dokos which is today uninhabited, is situated between the Saronic and the Argolic Gulfs. Spetses, as we mentioned, lies at the entrance of the Argolic Gulf, a gulf which belongs exclusively to the Peloponnese. The Argolic Gulf took its name from the historic city of Argos, which is near Nafplion.

Here we shall go on a tour of beautiful Aegina and idyllic Angistri.

Aegina

egina, in the centre of the Argosaronic, immediately conquers the visitor. One can see this for oneself as soon as one confronts its enchanting port, with its crowd of colourful boats and the old houses along the pier. A walk around the town will lead to many historical buildings dating from the 19th century. Among them is the house of Capodistrias, the first Governor of Greece after the War of Independence in 1821. It has remained standing to remind us that Aegina was for two years the temporary capital city of Greece, before it was officially installed in Nafplion. A stroll near the port will bring the visitor to the archaeological site of Kolonas. Here where the ancient city was built, when Aegina, with its powerful fleet, ruled the seas, long before Athens began to make its presence felt. Once the visitor has completed his or her trip around the town of Aegina, then the tour of the island will begin. At the foot of Oros, the tallest mountain on Aegina, he or she will 'discover' the sanctuary of Zeus Hellanios founded, according to the myth, by Aiakos, son of Zeus and grandfather of the heroes of the Trojan War Achilles and Ajax.

The visitor will discover the island's beautiful sands as he or she follows the coastal road southwards in the direction of the pretty fishing village of Perdikas. And he or she will be able to enjoy the indented coastline and the luscious-green northern coasts when travelling towards Souvala, the island's second port. The route that will remain unforgettable, though, is the one which passes the Monastery of Ayios Nektarios and the medieval village of Palaiochora, to arrive at the famous Temple

Oposite page:
The pine trees
reaching down to the
sea are quintessential
of Aegina.

Right: The port
of Aegina.

of Aphaia. Here, on a verdant hill on the north-eastern edge of the island, one can marvel at the temple that is considered to be the forerunner of the Parthenon. The route ends below at the bay of Ayia Marina (St Marina), the island's largest summer resort with its beautiful sandy beach and calm waters. Aegina is charming, with the mildest climate in the whole of Greece, many interesting sights and very good tourism facilities, offering the visitor a pleasant and eventful stay. And it has one further great advantage: it is only one hour by boat from the port of Piraeus.

Geography

Aegina is the second largest island in the Argosaronic - the largest being Salamis - and it is located almost in the centre of the Saronic Gulf. It has an area of 85 square kilometres, a coastline of 57 kilometres, and is 16 nautical miles from Piraeus. The island has over 11,000 permanent residents, over half of whom live in the town of Aegina. The luscious-green little island of Angistri is 4 nautical miles to the south-west of the port of Aegina. Very close to Aegina's south-west edge is the small picturesque islet of Moni.

Morphology

Aegina is shaped almost like an equilateral triangle, with each side having a length of nearly 12 kilometres. It has low mountain ranges, many of which are covered in pine forests. Its highest mountain is Oros, also known as Profitis Ilias, with an altitude of 532 metres. Its eastern and southern coasts are precipitous - with the exception of the large gulf of Ayia Marina - whilst the remaining coasts are flatter, with small and large gulfs. The climate is the mildest in all of Greece.

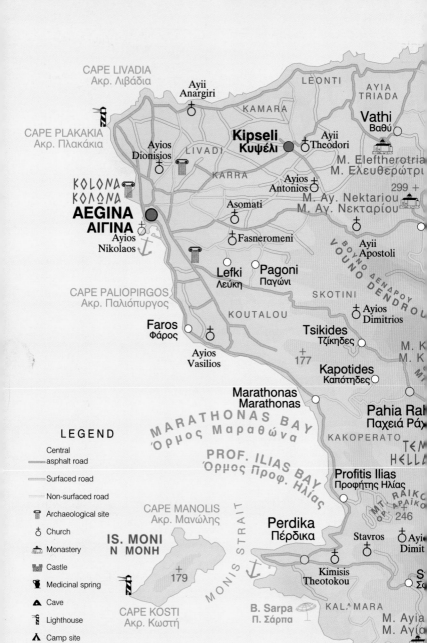

CAPE LIVADIA
Ακρ. Λιβάδια

Ayii
Anargiri

LEONTI

AYIA
TRIADA

KAMARA

Vathi
Βαθύ

CAPE PLAKAKIA
Ακρ. Πλακάκια

Ayios
Dionisios

LIVADI

Kipseli
Κυψέλι

Ayii
Theodori

M. Eleftherotria
M. Ελευθερώτρι

ΚΟΛΟΝΑ
ΚΟΛΩΝΑ
AEGINA
ΑΙΓΙΝΑ

KARRA

Ayios
Antonios

Asomati

M. Αγ. Nektariou
M. Αγ. Νεκταρίου

299 +

Ayios
Nikolaos

Fasneromeni

Ayii
Apostoli

Lefki
Λεύκη

Pagoni
Παγώνι

SKOTINI

CAPE PALIOPIRGOS
Ακρ. Παλιόπυργος

KOUTALOU

Ayios
Dimitrios

Faros
Φάρος

Ayios
Vasilios

Tsikides
Τζίκηδες

177 +

Kapotides
Καπότηδες

M. K

Marathonas
Marathonas

MARATHONAS BAY
Όρμος Μαραθώνα

Pahia Rah
Παχειά Ράχ

KAKOPERATO

TE
HELLA

LEGEND

Central
asphalt road

Surfaced road

Non-surfaced road

Archaeological site

Church

Monastery

Castle

Medicinal spring

Cave

Lighthouse

Camp site

Beach

Anchorage

PROF. ILIAS BAY
Όρμος Προφ. Ηλίας

CAPE MANOLIS
Ακρ. Μανώλης

IS. MONI
Ν ΜΟΝΗ

179 +

CAPE KOSTI
Ακρ. Κωστή

Profitis Ilias
Προφήτης Ηλίας

Perdika
Πέρδικα

Stavros

Ayi
Dimit

MT.
ΟΡ. ΡΑΪΚΟ
246

Kimisis
Theotokou

B. Sarpa
Π. Σάρπα

KALAMARA

M. Αγία
M. Αγία

B. Klima
Π. Κλήμα

CAPE Πί
Ακρ. Πί

Historica

The temple of Aphaia, 1820, painting by Hugh William Williams.

ntroduction

Mythology

Aegina has a special place in Greek mythology as it is believed that it is from here that the generation of the heroes of the Trojan War began. It is said that the island took its name from the most beautiful of the twenty daughters of the river god Asopos. Zeus, first among the gods, fell in love with this girl, who was called Aegina. He secretly kidnapped her from her father and led her to the then deserted Saronic island of Oinoni or Oinopia (island of wine, oinos = wine). Here they had Aiakos together. Aiakos, as soon as he became King, changed the name of the island to Aegina in honour of his mother. But he found himself in a place which did not have a single soul, and was thus forced to ask for help from his father. Zeus transformed the ants (in Greek, myrmingia) of the island into people and granted them to Aiakos. The people who lived on the island were called Myrmidons, a name reminiscent of the word 'myrmingia.'

Aiakos had two sons with Endeis, Peleus and Telamon, and later, with, Psamanthi, Phokos. Aiakos' two eldest sons were jealous of their halfbrother, who was better at athletic competitions than they. One day, in a stone-throwing competition, they killed him by throwing a stone over him. They left the island immediately, shocked and remorseful at their action. Peleus went to Thessaly and Telamon to the neighbouring island of Salamis, from where he desperately tried to contact his father and seek his forgiveness. Aiakos remained unrelenting and did not permit his son to return to the island. For this he gained the respect and admiration of the people and the gods, who made him a judge of the dead in Hades, along with Minos and Rhadamanthys. This highly interesting section on the mythology of Aegina can be brought to a close with the birth of two of the heroes of the Trojan War: Achilles, son of Peleus and Thetis, and Ajax, son of Telamon and Eriboea.

Vase representing the marriage of Thetis and Peleus, ca 570 BC. Museum of Florence.

Aegina was occupied in the later neolithic period (5th millennium BC), as we can see from the finds from the archaeological sites of Kolonas and Mesagros, near the Temple of Aphaia.

The first inhabitants came to the island from the coasts of the Peloponnese opposite. A second colonisation of the island took place in the 3rd millennium BC, this time by colonists from the Aegean. The Achaeans came to the island later (2000-1600 BC). It was then that the Aeginetans began to develop great naval and commercial activities and compete with the Minoans, who however succeeded in prevailing on the waters and in trade (1600-1200 BC).

The first silver coin depicting a turtle on one side.

During the same period the Myrmidons, a people originating from Thessaly, arrived on Aegina, settling in the area of Oros, the island's highest mountain. It is said that it was the Myrmidons who founded the sanctuary of Zeus Hellanios.

The Dorians arrived on Aegina around 950 BC, they were absorbed by the older residents and, all in common, they began once more to develop trade and shipping. There was continuous growth from this point on. Aegina was a member of the Kalaurian League (7th century BC), in which the fellow members were seven of the largest cities of ancient Greece, the centre of which was the sanctuary of Kalauria, today's Poros. Its ships travelled from the Black Sea to Egypt, shipping commercial goods. In order to conduct its commercial exchanges, Aegina was the first city in Greece to mint its own coins. These coins were silver and had a turtle on one side.

Wonderful new buildings and sanctuaries were built at the city of Kolonas, whilst the arts flourished. Sculpture in particular did well, and the school of 'Aeginetan Art,' as it has been called, included top-rate sculptors.

In the period when Aegina was flourishing most, the danger of invasion by the Persians was real. Fearing that their involvement in the Persian War would lead to their commercial relations with Asia Minor being cut off completely, the Aeginetans initially decided not to support the other Greeks against the Persians. This did not much please the Athenians who, after the Greek victory at Marathon (490 BC) attempted, unsuccessfully, to overthrow the oligarchic regime of Aegina.

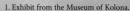

1. Exhibit from the Museum of Kolona.
2. The only surviving column (kolona) from the temple of Apollo, from which the area took its name.
3. The temple of Afaia.

The Aeginetans eventually took part in the Battle of Salamis (480 BC), putting up a fierce battle indeed. This fact was not enough to later prevent the Athenians, who had already grown into a great marine power, from occupying Aegina in 459 BC and forcing the island to pay a tribute. This was also the end of the island's peak period. The Athenians, at the beginning of the Peloponnesian War (431 BC), expelled the Aeginetans from the island and replaced them with what was known as a cleruchy, i.e. they settled the island with Athenians. The Aeginetans were returned to the island by the Spartans when the latter won the Peloponnesian War (404 BC).

Aegina came under the control of Pergamon for a period, and was later conquered by the Romans, who held it from 133 BC until the early Byzantine period in the mid-4th century AD. The centuries which passed were marked by foreign raids by Goths, Avars, etc. The most serious was the fierce attack of the Saracenes in the 9th century, which forced the residents of Kolonas to abandon their city and to build a new one, today's Palaiochora, in the centre of the island. This city, its many churches reminiscent of Mystras, experienced prosperity for several centuries.

The end of the long Byzantine period was signalled by the capture of Constantinople by the Franks (Western Europeans) in 1204. The 'Frangokratia', period of Frankish rule, ensued on the island. Later came the 'Enetokratia' (Venetian rule), to be substituted twice by the 'Tourkokratia', Turkish rule, which lasted until the War of Independence in 1821. The most significant event during the clashes between the Venetians and the Turks was the destruction of the island by the Turkish pirate Khair-ed-Din Barbarossa in 1537, and the raiding and pillaging by the Venetian Morosini in 1654. Aegina played an important role during the struggle for freedom which began in 1821, and in 1828 it became the capital city of a free Greece. The first Governor, Ioannis Capodistrias, settled here in the Governor's House, or the Palace of Barba-Yiannis (Uncle John, in reference to Capodistrias), as the people called it. Here Capodistrias began the building of a new Greece. The visitor can see the Governor's House even today, along with all the other public works which survive on the island.

1. The church of Episkopi at Palaiochora.
2. Bust of Ioannis Capodistrias.
3. The Governor's Residence (or House of Capodistrias).

Culture &

tradition

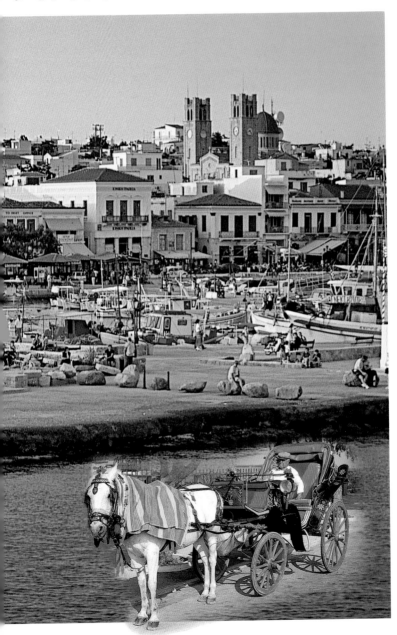

Customs

*T*he passage of time and the closer relationship with Athens resulted in the local customs fading away or even dying out completely. The most important of the local customs, the wedding, however, still survives in various forms, mainly in the villages. It is a ritual which lasts for days.

The wedding starts with the display of the bride's dowry, which is sprinkled with rice. The 'making of the bed' then follows, and the giving of gifts accompanied by songs and best wishes for the bride and the groom. The church service usually takes place on a Sunday, with the wedding feast in the evening, with musical instruments, dance and song. A feast which in the old days lasted for three days. The folk instruments which were used years ago at all the feasts and festivals were the violin, the lute and the dulcimer, whilst most of the songs that were heard were rhyming couplets, the lyric depending on the occasion. We have wedding songs such as the following:

"I'll sing you one song on the cherry
May the couple just brought together live long, grow old."

We also have Easter carnival songs, feast songs, and songs of the sea which the Aeginetans call 'voyes' and which are of especial interest. These were the songs that were used to synchronise the pace at which oars were rowed, before they were replaced by engines, or the rhythm of the steps of the fishermen as they hauled at the trawl nets. So, we have the voya of the oar and the voya of the trawl net, such as this one by Yiannis Yiannitsaris::

"Yia lesa, yia lesa. Let the trawl come in.
Yia lesa and it's getting dark and the cauldron is boiling."

As for the dances of Aegina, they are similar to other island dances, such as the group dance of the syrtos (especially 'The mountains of Palaiochora') and the ballo, danced by couples, as well as other dances, such as the sousta and the kalamatianos.

The island's largest festival is on 15 August at the Monastery of the Chrysoleontissa, which attracts huge crowds. The largest religious gathering takes place on 9 November at the Monastery of Ayios Nektarios, when celebrations take place in memory of the Saint. This festival attracts the faithful not just from the island but from all over Greece.

$\mathcal{T}$he Aeginetans may love the sea, but this does not mean that they were never engaged in agriculture, something which they are still involved in. The island has many cultivated areas, the use of which during wars and especially during the last centuries of the Tourkokratia was absolutely necessary.

In addition to these main occupations - to which we must also add **sponge-diving**, which had disappeared by the mid-20th century - there were two other occupations on the island, which are also slowly disappearing. These are pottery and lace-making.

Examples of local pottery and lace-making production.

Pottery is an ancient tradition on Aegina, continuing until our days. Indeed, in the years just before the Second World War, this trade had developed to such an extent that pottery was even exported. This was when the famous Aeginetan jugs with their colourful external decoration were produced.

These jugs were in great demand, not just for storing water, but also because of their porous walls through which a small amount of water could seep and keep the outside of the jug damp. When this water evaporated, then, the walls of the jug were cooled thus keeping its contents cool as well. These jugs were usually placed on the sill of an open window. The results were both quicker and better using this method, whilst the elegant jugs on the window sills would add a note of charm to the little lanes.

The arrival of the electric refrigerator saw the end of the Aeginetan jugs. The 'kanatades' - jug-makers - dwindled and today there remain only a few potters. And these potters no longer make jugs, but various ceramic wares to be sold to the tourists.

The art of **lace-making** was taught to the women of Aegina around 120 years ago by a foreign lady from western Europe. This technique was known as 'kopaneli' and was used to make table-cloths, doilies, centrepieces, etc.

It is a finely-worked form of embroidery which demands much time and effort, and for this reason the product is quite pricey, making it difficult to sell.

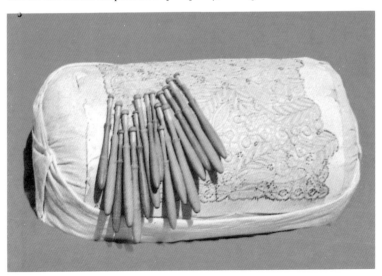

Local produces

Aegina produces mainly olives, raisons, almonds, and, of course, pistachios, the cultivation of which started 100 years ago, for it to finally become the most profitable produce.

Many of the small plains and footfills of the island are covered in pistachio nut trees. The famed «Aegina pistachio» (the official name of the tree is the genuine Pistakia, i.e. *Pistacia vera*) is one of the island's main items of produce.

It was first brought to Aegina in 1860 from Syria by Peroglou, whilst the first person to cultivate it was Christos Moiras from Kypseli. the tree's origins meant that the Aegina pistachio resembled that of Syria, in other words it was round like a hazelnut. Once in Aegina, however, the tree began to evolve and the shape of the nut changed, the island's clay soil making it exceptionally tasty.

Architecture
Sculpture

When talking about yesterday and today, we should certainly mention the ancient years, which gave Aegina such a rich cultural heritage. How can we not mention that the famous Aeginetan sculptors Kallon and Onatos, once they had finished carving the famous statues on the pedin.ents of the Temple of Aphaia, helped - or so it is said - Pheidias in carving the Parthenon sculptures. It is also said that the technique used by these sculptors was a precursor for the creation of the Parthenon and of the shift from the archaic to the classical period.

This was the 'Aeginetan Art,' which began in the archaic period and a leading figure of which was Smilis, a figure who is said to have been active in both Aegina and Samos and who may very well have been a mythical character. Smilis was followed by many brilliant artists, among them Kallon, creator of the west pediment of the Temple of Aphaia, and Onatos, creator of the later and finer east pediment of the Temple. Onatos was the last and also the greatest of the artists of the 'Aeginetan Workshop.'

1. Head of Ajax. West pediment of the temple of Aegina. 505-500 BC. Munich Glyptothek.
2. Head of Athena. West pediment of the temple of Aegina. 505-500 BC. Munich Glyptothek.
3. Representation of Aphaia from the west. Munich Glyptothek.
4. East side of the temple of Aphaia, today.

3

4

1. The once stunning mansion of Voyiatzis.
2. Typical example of church architecture from Aegina.
3. The church of the Panayitsa.

The centuries passed, the ancient city of Aegina was abandoned, and the Aeginetans created Palaiochora, another Mystra with its Byzantine churches. Palaiochora was also aban-doned in the 19th century, for the capital city to be transferred once more close to the sea, on the same site as before. Of course, this new town did not have anything in common with the old. It did not have its grand public buildings, there were no temples and famous sculptures.

Even so, as far as architecture goes, 19th-century Aegina was pioneering, and it was from here that the neo-classical style began. The start was made in 1828 when Aegina became the capital of liberated Greece and the first Governor, Capodistrias, assisted by Greek and foreign architects, began to erect the first public buildings.

The imposing building of the Orphanage, with its simple Doric design, is considered as one of the first examples of the neo-classical style, and was subsequently repeated on other buildings in the town. This style later spread to Athens, and it became the dominant architectural style for a century. We will discuss the protected neo-classical buildings of Aegina town in more detail in the next section.

With the passing of time the official architecture of Aegina gave way to a popular architectural style, which on general lines can be considered as part of the broader 'Aegean Sea' style, yet with its own distinct character and particularities. The white of the villages of the Aegean has been replaced by soft and warm colours, which better match the idyllic environment of the island. This combination is today most noticeable in the town and port of Aegina.

Here, as the sun sets, the peaceful waters of the sea take on a golden colour and the sky reddens. The beautiful landscape foregrounds the traditional houses and the plethora of boats moored at the jetties. Most of these are fishing boats, highlighting the close ties between the people of the island and the sea. Ties which have their roots in the ancient years, then when Aegina dominated trade and shipping, and was Athens' main rival.

Arts and Letters

efore closing this brief journey through yesterday and today, we should mention the great contribution of Aeginetans to the arts and letters. The contribution of the distinguished sculptors H. Kapralos (who was born in Agrinio but active in Aegina), N. Klonos and V. Antoniou; the painters F. Kappos, K. Galaris, Kontovrakis, and others; the photographer Y. Mairis; the historians and folklorists P. Ireiotis and Y. Kouliakourdis; the poets N. Lievas, A. Kyriakopoulos, A. Androutsos, K. Sarantakos and others; and the female poet T. Katsimingou-Yiannouli, a poem of whose we quote here:

4

DEDICATION TO AEGINA
In your blue waters, which roll slowly
and to the beautiful red-golden evenings,
to your magical coasts, which talk
with bright, fairytale-like evenings.

1, 2. Lanes in Perdika and Aegina town.
3. View of Aegina, lithograph by Karl Krazeisen, 1826.
4. «'The Mother', sculpture by Ch. Kaprolos.

The town and the

surrounding areas

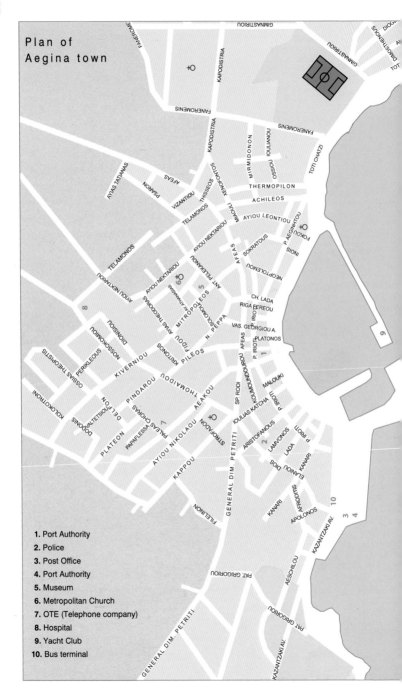

Plan of Aegina town

1. Port Authority
2. Police
3. Post Office
4. Port Authority
5. Museum
6. Metropolitan Church
7. OTE (Telephone company)
8. Hospital
9. Yacht Club
10. Bus terminal

*A*s soon as the boat passes the lighthouse and archaeological site of Kolonas, on the north-west coast of the island, then the town and port of Aegina suddenly appear. The town, clambering up the green hills, and the port, with the long row of two- and three-storey houses in front of the dock. A crowd of all kinds of boats painted in all sorts of colours moored at the jetties round of this pretty picture.

The brilliant-white church of **Ayios Nikolaos Thalassinos** stands out at the entrance to the port, on a wide jetty to the right. This church, with its two domes, is reminiscent of the Cyclades and is, we could say, the 'trademark' of Aegina.

To the right, another jetty, narrower than the first, starts from the church of the **Panayitsa**, the imposing church on the right edge of the port. This jetty terminates at the kiosk of the Nautical Circle, opposite the church of Ayios Nikolaos. This point here, where the two jetties meet, is the entrance to the port.

The port of Aegina is wide, built on the site of the ancient commercial port. The ancient military harbour, as we shall see, is further to the north. On the eastern side of the port there is another mole, where ferryboats and speed boats dock.

This point is dominated by the large **mansion of Voyiatzis**, which has been described as a work of art, as have many other buildings. Opposite Voyiatzis' mansion, in the shadow of some large trees, is the square with the taxi and one-horse carriage rank. These are the carriages drawn along by one horse, dressed in multi-coloured costume.

These carriages are the traditional means of transport, a means which fits perfectly with the layout of the town and adds to its charm. Many people prefer the carriages to the taxis.

Opposite the taxi rank is Eleftherias Square, near which is the **mansion of Kanaris**.

A walk along the waterfront is a delight. The wide coastal road, with much space for pedestrians to walk next to the sea, runs in both directions for wheeled vehicles, and for this reason there is a small dividing lane in the centre. On the side of the sea, the old buildings stand in a row with cafes, patisseries and shops on the ground floors, all competing with each other as to which is the most delightful. All have canopies laid out in front to protect the patrons from the sun, as well as the goods which are displayed on the pavement. Of course, among all these goods is the Aegina pistachio, the celebrated local produce, which only in Aegina do they know how to produce so well. Packaged in cellophane so as to protect the contents, it stands out either on its own or amongst the other products.

Somewhere in the middle of the port on the main road is the elegant neo-classical **Town Hall** building. Opposite this, in from of the sea, a unique, one might say, sight draws the attention of the visitor. This is an improvised fruit market set up on the caiques, which are loaded with various tasty fruits. Many of their crates are placed one next to the other on the dock, an extension of those already in the caiques.

1. Ayios Nikolaos Thalassinos.
2. The Town Hall.
3. The one-horse carriages are a typical sight on Aegina.

3

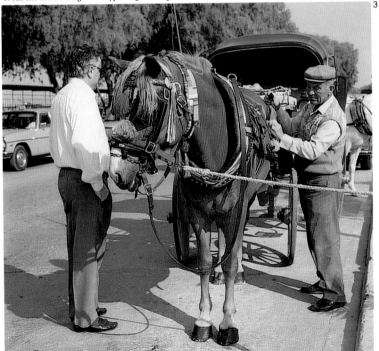

The south edge of the port is dominated, as we said, by the **church of the Panayitsa**. Next to it, inside a small park, is a marble statue of Capodistrias (see p. 23), the first Governor of Greece after the Revolution of 1821.

1. The tower of Markellos.
2. The Metropolitan church.
3. The church of Panayitsa.

The rest of the town, particularly the centre, is also of great interest. Most of the tavernas are to be found on the first road parallel to the port, and on the second road parallel with Aphaias Street, an extension of Spyridon Roidis Street. The **Folk Museum** is also here, as well as the few remaining pottery shops, which sold the traditional clay jugs. Those which kept the water cool in the days when there were no fridges. Today, instead of jugs, they sell various ceramic wares.

Proceeding further into the town, we encounter the **Tower of Markellos** in an open space. This is a medieval building which was used by the first Greek government after the Revolution of 1821. Near this Tower there is yet another building, of great importance for modern Greek history. This is the **Government House**, the **house of Capodistrias**, the first Governor of a free Greece, from which he governed the country for two years after its independence, when Aegina was the temporary capital of Greece.

Next to the house of Capodistrias is the **Public Library**. A little to the south is the **Metropolitan Church**, an old church with three red domes and three large arches over its facade, upon which the roof of the forecourt is supported.

To the south-west of the centre of the town, behind a football pitch, there stands a large building. This is the **Orphanage**, built during Capodistrias' rule, which functioned both as a home and a school for orphans.

Public services were housed in this building, and it was then converted into a prison, which later closed. So, today it stands empty, awaiting its next use. Faneromenis Street, which passes along the Orphanage, proceeds towards the **Monastery of the Faneromeni**, where there is a semi-dilapidated 13th-century church and two smaller churches. To the south of the city, near the cemetery, there is another 19th-century mansion. This belonged to Harilaos Trikoupis, one of the great Greek prime ministers of the later 19th century.

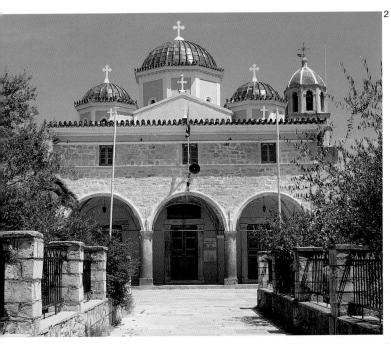

The cathedral church of the Ayii Theodorii (SS Theodore), the so-called **'Beautiful Church,'** is located to the east of the town, near the neighbourhood of the Ayii Asomati and at a distance of around 2 km. from the port. It is perhaps the most

important surviving church of Aegina, built in the late 13th century. Its interior is full of well-preserved wall paintings.

After Eleftherias Square, the coastal road proceeds in a north-west direction and passes the coast of Avra. Some say that this is where the military harbour of ancient Aegina was, although according to

others it was located at the next bay. The ancient military harbour was excellently organised, with very good installations which it is said could hold as many as sixty triremes. Immediately after this coast and behind a small park is the hill with the archaeological site of Kolonas and the Museum (see below). The sandy beach of Kolonas stretches out behind the archaeological site, and this beach is the most busy of all those near the town.

The coastal road continues to the neighbourhood of **Plakakia**, with its beautiful villas, amongst which stand out the **Zaimis Tower** and the Benizelos house within a large garden with palm trees.

After the Zaimis Tower the road continues along the north-west edge of Aegina, with its picturesque lighthouse and the little church of the Ayii Apostoli (Holy Apostles).

The austere and simple house in which Nikos Kazantzakis - the internationally-acclaimed Greek novelist upon whose

1. The Kapralos Museum.
2. Kazantzakis' house.
3. The tower of Zaimis.

book 'The Life and Times of Alexis Zorbas' the film 'Zorba the Greek' was based - lived is a little past the lighthouse. The **Kapralos Museum** is a short distance from Kazantzakis' house. The great sculptor's works, dating from 1963 until his death in 1993, are exhibited here. It is said that the large sculpture entitled 'Mother' and situated outside the museum next to the sea represents the artist's own peasant mother (see page 37).

The archaeological site of Kolona

$\mathcal{E}$xcavations at the archaeological site of Kolona were first carried out by Furtwaengler and Lolling, becoming more systematic under G.Welter in the period 1921-1954. Between 1966-1992 they were conducted by the Bavarian Academy under the direction of Professor H. Walter and, from 1994 under F. Felten for the Austrian Archaeological Institute.

This is a very important archaeological site, not simply because of the ruins of the famous temple of Apollo and other buildings, but because it contains the remains of ten successive prehistoric settlements dating from the late neolithic period (5th millennium BC) until the Mycenean period (1600-1200 BC).

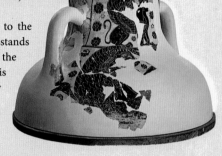

All the finds are gathered on a hill to the north of the port, at the peak of which stands a single column (kolona), from which the hill took its name. The column, which is part of the temple of Apollo, is the only one which has remained upright of the eleven which stood on each of the long sides and the six on each of the short sides. The temple was built in the late

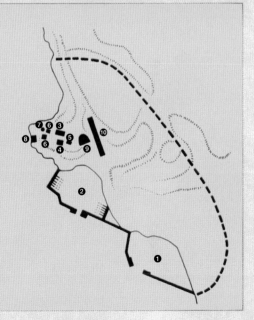

View of
ancient Aegina

1. Commercial harbour
2. Military harbour
3. Temple of Apollo
4. Aiakeion
5. Bouleuterion (council house)
6. Two unknown tombs
7. Tomb of Phokos
8. Attaleion
9. Theatre
10. Stadium

6th century BC and dominated the region due to its size and its beauty which was equal, it is said, to that of the Temple of Aphaia, which we shall see below.

The foundations of some other structures belonging to the temple have also survived, such as the altar to the east of the temple, the Temple of Artemis to the south-east, two small rectangular buildings and a circular one.

Views of the ruins of the archaeological site of Kolona.

There are also the remains of many walls from different eras, such as the Bronze Age fortress walls, the archaic acropolis walls, the Roman sanctuary walls, and the so-called port walls which run down towards the port.

Other significant remains are those of a rectangular structure which was perhaps used as a gathering place and which Pindar refers to as a viewing gallery.

The Museum of Kolona

The Museum of Kolonas is located in front of the site in a new, square one-storey building with a large atrium in the centre. The atrium contains sculptures from the cemetery of Reneia, from the time that Capodistrias brought them to Aegina. The splendid large and narrow hall of the museum contains some fine exhibits dating from the late neolithic period until the Roman period.

Among the finds are red-buff vases with painted decoration and small clay idols from the earliest prehistoric settlement (5th millennium BC), Bronze Age pottery (3rd millennium BC), such as the 'gravy boats' which stand out for their perfect technique, as well as Middle Bronze Age (2000 - 1600 BC) items, such as buff-grey painted vases and other Minoan-type vases. There are a large number of pottery items from the Mycenean period, whilst the archaic (7th - 6th century BC) vases are important too, such as the Ram Jug representing Odysseus and his companions escaping from the Cyclops.

The archaic and early classical periods are also represented by the famous marble sphinx of Aegina (460 BC) as well as sculptures from the pediment of the Temple of Apollo. The sculpture of Herakles is most probably from the pediment of the earlier limestone temple, whilst the tombstone with relief sculpture dates to the late 5th century.

At the entrance to the museum are the impressive models of a house from the prehistoric city III on the hill of Kolonas, the so-called 'white house,' and of a bronze-foundry. The models make quite clear that the 'white house' had two floors. The foundry dates to around 2300 BC, whilst the 'white house' dates to around 2200 BC.

Exhibits from the museum of Kolona.

the island

Aerial photograph in which
Souvala and Kypseli can be seen.

This route mainly covers the northern edge of the island, which is the most densely-populated. From the house of Kazantzakis and the Kapralos Museum the road continues for Souvala. This is the quickest route from the town of Aegina, and goes to Souvala via Kypseli.

Kypseli is the island's second-largest town which is almost merged with the capital. The brilliant-white old domed church of Ayios Moulos can be seen from afar between this road and the coastal one, set on a verdant height. The large, pretty square of Kypseli, dominated by the beautiful church of the Evangelismos (when the Archangel Gabriel told Mary that she was going to give birth to the Son of God), is about 4 km. from the town of Aegina. The road continues for the village of Vathy and then descends to reach, after another 4 km., Souvala, the harbour of Vathy and the island's second port.

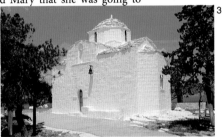

Souvala is known for its hot springs which can help with arthritis, rheumatism, skin problems and gynaecological problems. It is also a tourist centre and there are regular direct connections with Piraeus. The large docks, with the fishermen's nets spread out and the plethora of fishing and tourist boats impress. There are hotels,

1. The central square with the church of the Evangelismos at Kypseli.
2. The port at Souvala.
3. Ayios Nikolaos Moulos at Kypseli.
4. The little port at Vaia.

and many apartments and rented rooms to meet the needs of visitors. A very interesting trip can be made from Souvala. This goes up to Palaiochora and the Monastery of Ayios Nektarios, and meets the central arterial road from Aegina through Aphaia and Ayia Marina, which we shall read more about below.

The coastal road continues in an easterly direction and passes alongside the luscious-green Ayii, to reach, after 3.5 km., **Vaia,** yet another small tourist resort, smaller than Souvala, with a pretty little port.

From Vaia, as from Souvala, a road rises towards Mesagros and the central arterial road of Aegina-Aphaia-Ayia Marina.

Ayios Nektarios
Monastery

Palaiochora

Chrysoleontissa
Monastery

This route is the first section of the one of the largest and most important routes throughout the island. You can start from Aphaias Street, which begins at the centre of the port and which is the second parallel road with the port. You can also start on this route from other roads further to the south, which all finally meet up with Aphaias Street.

The road cuts across the town of Aegina and continues in an easterly direction towards the island's hinterland. The houses become sparser and sparser, to be replaced by fields with beautiful country churches and lots of greenery. The nature here is serene, with nothing out of the ordinary, and the smooth lines

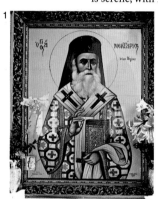

of the mountains create an atmosphere of calm. Yet, the first surprise comes after a distance of about 5.5 km.

An imposing church with two tall belfries and four rows of windows with red arches, suddenly appears on the left of the road. This is Ayios Nektarios, a new church built below the **Monastery of Ayios Nektarios**, the architecture of which is reminiscent of that of Ayia Sophia in Constantinople. This nunnery, the entrance to which is on the road for Souvala and very near to the crossing with the Aegina-Aphaia arterial route, was built at the beginning of the 20th

1. 2. The church of Ayios Nektarios and the icon of the saint. 3. The Monastery of Ayia Aikaterini with Palaiochora behind.

century on the site of a small Byzantine monastery dedicated to the Zoodochos Pigi (life-giving source) by the Bishop of Pentapoli Nektarios.

Ayios Nektarios passed the last years of his life in the monastery, carrying out a great philanthropical work and gaining the admiration and adoration of the faithful, who flocked to the monastery to meet him. Many still talk about his generosity and his ability to cure people suffering from incurable diseases. Ayios Nektarios died in 1920 and was buried in the monastery. He was canonised in 1961.

From then on the monastery, which had been known as the Monastery of Ayios Theodoros, was renamed the Monastery of Ayios Nektarios. The Saint's memory is celebrated on 9 November, when thousands of faithful gather at the monastery, having come from all parts of Greece.

On the right of the road which goes from the church of Ayios Nektarios to Souvala, and before the entrance to the Monastery, is the small, brilliant-white **nunnery of Ayia Aikaterini**, surrounded by vegetation, the tall cypress trees standing out.

The iconostasis in the church of Ayios Nektarios at Palaiochora.

View of Palaichora

1. Ayios Charalambos
2. Stavros
3. Panayia of Yiannouli
4. Ayia Varvara
5. Ayios Georgios
   the Catholic
6. Episkopi
7. Ayios Nikolaos
8. Ayía Anna
9. Ayii Theodori
10. Ayios Eleftherios
11. Ayios Minas

12. Ayia Marina
13. Ayia Kyriaki
14. Ayii Dimitrios and Georgios
15. Well
16. Taxiarchis Michael
17. Ayios Ioannis Theologos
18. Ayios Nikolaos
19. Ayii Anargyri
20. Ayia Ekaterini
21. Kimisi tis Miteras
    tis Theotokou
22. Ayios Dimitrios
23. Kimisi tis Theotokou

24. Taxiarchis
25. Metamorphosis
26. Ayios Euthemios
27. Ayios Ioannis
28. Ayios Georgios
29. Ayios Stefanos
30. Ayios Athanasios
31. Ayios Kyrikos
32. Ayios Stylianos
33. Ayios Zacharias
34. Ayía Kryfti
35. Ayios Spyridonas
36. Ruins
37. Chapel

This same road, as it ascends, winds around a rocky hill on its right. Some grey-yellow buildings can be seen scattered around on this hill. These are the approximately 35 of the many churches that existed in Palaiochora (tradition says there were 365) which remain standing. Around 20 of these still have some fine wall-paintings preserved.

Palaiochora is another Mystras. It began to be built in 896 after a fierce raid by Saracene pirates on the coastal town of Aegina. Centuries later it became the capital of the island, to be abandoned at the beginning of the 19th century when the inhabitants slowly began to return to the sea and rebuild the new Aegina.

The ruins of Palaiochora are approached from a pass in the hills, there where the ascent of the road towards Souvala ends. At this point is the church of Stavros, the first church which the visitor to Palaiochora will meet.

From here the footpaths which follow the old paved roads lead to the old Byzantine churches, such as Panayia of Yiannouli and Ayios Georgios the Catholic. During the period of Catalan rule this church belonged to the Catholics, but was later again restored to the Orthodox. Other churches include Episkopi, the metropolitan church of Palaiochora, in which the Bishop of Aegina Dionysius, later saint of Zakynthos, officiated (his cell is preserved next to the church), the Taxiarchis (Archangel), a cruciform church, the Ayii Theodori, etc.

After Episkopi, a diversion to the left from the main path leads, after an uphill walk for fifteen minutes, to the Kastro, the castle, built by the Venetians in the 17th century.

The hill of Palaiochora with the many churches.

At the peak there are preserved two small churches, built next to each other. These are Ayios Georgios and Ayios Dimitrios. There are the ruins of walls, houses and wells on the Kastro, and the view from here, especially towards the beach of Souvala, is exceptional.

After the visit to Palaiochora, you can continue your route on the main road towards Aphaia and Ayia Marina, or go in a northerly direction towards Souvala. There is yet another road in a southerly direction, leading from the new church of Ayios Nektarios in the hamlet of Kontos. This road is three kilometres long and provides the opportunity for a visit to the important **Monastery of the Chrysoleontissa**. The monastery is located in the centre of the island, and it dominates from high up on the luscious-green mountain slopes. The road terminates at a mountain range, from which point we can reach the monastery after a walk of about fifteen minutes. The monastery, with tall fortress-like walls, was built at the beginning of the 17th century so that the old monastery at Leonti on the north coast of the island could be moved to a safer place and escape from the relentless pirate raids. It is a large two-storey building with a courtyard in the centre. In the courtyard there is a church and, next to it, a tall three-storey tower. The church is newer and was built on the site of the

older one, which was destroyed in a fire. The icon of the Panayia (Virgin Mary) is well-worth seeing. The Aeginitans all bow with respect to this icon. The church's iconostasis and wall-paintings are also of interest. The Monastery, which celebrates its feast day on 15 August, when the island's largest festival takes place, converted in 1935 from a male monastery to a female nunnery.

Left:
The entrance to the Bishop's Residence at Palaiochora.
1. The monastery of Panayia Chrysoleontissa.
2. The church of Ayii Theodori.

Mesagros

Aphaia

Ayia Marina

*T*he road from Ayios Nektarios leads in an easterly direction, nine miles from the town of Aegina, to **Mesagros**, a large hamlet with a few houses and whose inhabitants work in agriculture. The surrounding area has quite a bit of vegetation, including, of course, plenty of pistachios.

After Mesagros begins the ascent up a beautiful pine-clad hill, at the top of which is one of the most beautiful temples of ancient Greece, the **Temple of Aphaia**. It was not by chance that this spot was chosen as the location of the temple. The panoramic view from here over the charming gulf of Ayia Marina is outstanding. Moreover, traces of a later neolithic (3000 BC) settlement have been found. This settlement and Kolona are the oldest settlements on the island. Before the temple that we see today was built, two smaller temples had been constructed. The first was built in around 600 BC and only a small section of its foundations survive.

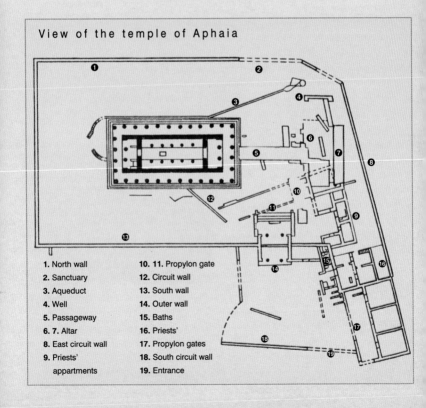

View of the temple of Aphaia

1. North wall
2. Sanctuary
3. Aqueduct
4. Well
5. Passageway
6. 7. Altar
8. East circuit wall
9. Priests' appartments
10. 11. Propylon gate
12. Circuit wall
13. South wall
14. Outer wall
15. Baths
16. Priests'
17. Propylon gates
18. South circuit wall
19. Entrance

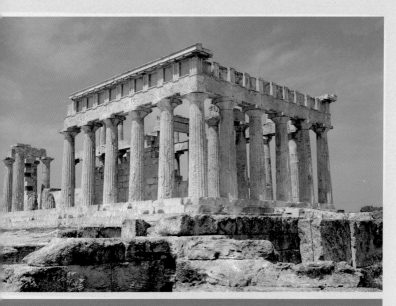

Only the altar survives from the second temple. The third temple to have been built, the one we see today, is an exceptional example of late archaic architecture. It is in the Doric order and was built with local limestone in around 500 BC. It had six columns on the short sides and twelve on the long sides. Twenty of these columns survive today, whilst in the cella (the main area of the temple) there were two internal colonnades parallel to the main colonnades, with five columns each. There was a second row of five smaller columns above, built in such a way as to form a stoa, in the form of a raised section around the three sides of the temple. The decoration on both the exterior as well as the interior was exceptional. What gave the temple its greatest splendour, however, were its famous pedimental sculptures. Unfortunately, however, these have suffered a similar fate to those of the Parthenon.

In 1811 the German Baron von Hallerstein and the English architect Cockerell, who discovered the sculptures after excavation, transported them to Zakynthos, which was then under British rule, and from there they went to Italy. They were then bought in an auction by Ludwig I, King of Bavaria, father of the future King of Greece Otto, who took them to the Glypthotek in Munich, where they remain. These sculptures include 16 statues carved from Parian marble and many other pieces.

These sculptures formed scenes from the Trojan War, with the goddess Athena as the central figure in both the pediments. As a result, it was initially believed that temple had been built in honour of Athena. During excavations carried out much later (in 1901), the German archaeologist Fürtwangler discovered an ancient description with the name of Aphaia. She was a local goddess, and tradition associates her with the Cretan Britomartis. According to the myth, Britomartis was the daughter of Zeus and half-sister of Artemis, who loved her greatly and took her hunting with her. Minos fell madly in love with Britomartis, and she sought refuge in the sea. As she jumped into the waters, her foot was caught up in the nets of some fishermen, who transported her to Aegina. Her

misfortunes were not to end here, though, as a fisherman tried to rape her. Artemis then intervened, and made Britomartis invisible and took her into the island's woods. In this way, then, Britomartis became 'aphanis,' or invisible. In the dialect of the time, this was pronounced 'aphaia.'

A section of the eastern pediment was destroyed a few years after the erection of the building. The shattered statues were buried, as was customary, and new ones put in their place. Thankfully, Fürtwangler was able to uncover them, so that the National Archaeological Museum in Athens could also have a piece, even a little one, of the famous sculptures of the Temple of Aphaia. Around the temple there are the remains of various buildings. Entrance to the archaeological site is through a small gateway. Straight ahead to the right are the ruins of the priests' houses and immediately after them are the baths. There follow the great gate and the path taken by the procession, beginning from the altar and reaching the entrance to the temple, which is in its east side. The temple was divided, as was the rule, into the pronaos, the cella - the main area of the temple which housed the goddess's statue - and the opisthodomos at the back.

The Temple of Aphaia is connected with the port of Aegina, 11.5 km. away, by coaches which depart from Ayia Marina. The archaeological site is open every day, except Mondays, from 8:30 to 17:00.

The temple of Aphaia.

From Aphaia, the road descends with many bends, to reach the pretty gulf of **Ayia Marina** after 4 kilometres. This was once a fishing village with two or three tavernas, but has today grown, thanks to its wonderful sands and dense pine forest, into a large tourist centre which in the summer bustles with life. Villas, hotels, restaurants, bars, an organised beach with facilities for water sports, and anything else the visitor could ask for, they will surely find in this resort.

The little harbour is full of boats small and large, whilst in the summer there are direct connections with Piraeus in small boats. From Ayia Marina the road, following the coast, continues on to the fishing port of Portes.

The return journey to the town of Aegina can be made through the settlement of Alones, with its small villas and restaurants, via a road which meets the main road at Mesagros, by-passing Aphaia.

The gulf of Ayia Marina.

Pacheia Rachi

Temple of
Zeus Hellanios

Portes

*T*his is another route of great interest, centring on an archaeological site that is directly connected with the mythology and history of Aegina. This route crosses the island from north-west to south-east, passing alongside **Oros**, Aegina's highest mountain. The road - Faneromenis Street - begins at the old prisons of Aegina and at first travels parallel with the coastal road. It turns left to Pacheia Rachi before meeting with the coastal road.

As this road ascends the view on the right over the sea becomes all the more beautiful. At first you can see the town of Aegina in the distance as it is left behind, whilst to the left is Angistri, luscious green and also in the distance.

The islet of Moni soon appears before the peninsula of Methana. A little further to the left, like a white line on a narrow strip of land which continues into the sea, is picturesque Perdika. The row of white houses on the beach down below belong to the village of Marathon. We shall have the chance to see all these from closer up on the last leg of our journey around the island.

The village of **Pacheia Rachi,** which looks out over the sea and the plain, soon appears. The belfry and blue dome of the

church stand out. Just beyond the village are the new facilities of Centre for the Care of Wild Animals and Birds, which is being relocated here from the former prisons of Aegina.

Every year the Centre takes care of many wounded (mainly by hunters) and sick wild animals and birds. The Centre is a very commendable effort by a group of young people whose aim is to care for these animals and then to return them to their natural environment.

1. The village Pachia Rachi.
2. Oros, Aegina's highest mountain.

Beyond the Centre, a dirt road to the right leads to Sfyrictres, and the archaeological site with the **sanctuary of Zeus Hellanios**. From a distance one can discern the broad, grand stone staircase next to a Hellenistic wall.

On the upper part of the staircase, to the left, is the Byzantine church of the Taxiarches, the Archangels, which used to be the cathedral church of a monastery. The ruins of the monks' cells can still be seen round about the church. The wall was most probably built in order to fill it in so as to create a large, flat, square area upon which the sanctuary of Zeus Hellanios was built.

Tradition has it that no rain fell on Aegina for many years, and the island suffered greatly. Aiakos, the mythical King of Aegina and son of Zeus, was advised by the oracle at Delphi to plead with his father to bring rainfall. His plea was heard and, in order to thank Zeus, Aiakos built this temple in the god's honour and established his cult here.

Today, from the south-east corner of this large terrace, and beneath some tall rocks, we can see the foundations of a large structure and the bases of three rows of columns, which supported the roof. It is likely that this structure acted as a hostel for pilgrims.

Further up, at a little distance from the terrace, there are two wells within the rocks and the large stones, which most likely were also created to serve the needs of the pilgrims. These wells, most likely fed by some spring, even today contain a little stagnant water, which is not, however, drinkable.

Above the temple stands the mountain with the ancient name of Oros, and which is directly associated with the cult of Zeus on the island. It has the shape of a cone and is covered in rocks and stones. The footpath leading up to its peak (532 m), the tallest in Aegina, is to the west. Traces of buildings have been found on the peak, and it was initially believed that they were part of the sanctuary of Zeus Hellanios. This is not the case, however, as these buildings date to the 13th century BC whilst it appears that the Dorians brought the cult of Zeus to Aegina in around 1000 BC.

1. Perdika and the islet of Moni from Marathon.
2. The church of Taxiarchis.
3. Ancient cisterns from the temple of Zeus Hellanios.
4. The sanctuary of Zeus Hellanios.

The view of the island and the whole of the Argosaronic from the peak of Mt Oros, today known as Profitis Ilias, is splendid. The small, brilliant-white church which stands here is not dedicated, as is usually the case, to the Prophet Elias but to the Analapsi, the Ascension of Christ.

From the crossing with the dirt road that leads to the sanctuary of Zeus Hellanios, the central road continues towards the east and soon starts to descend down to the sea, with many bends. There is much vegetation along this route, mainly pine and olive trees. A little house to the right of the road catches the eye. This is, in fact, an azure, two-storey mill with a conical blue roof. At the end of the road lies the isolated and serene fishing village of **Portes**, with its few houses and little taverna built on a rise. A beautiful pebbly beach stretches out to the right, whilst to the left, next to the road which leads to the north, is the small artificial harbour which protects the boats in the area.

1, 3. The beach and the mill-cum-house at Portes.
2. The beach between Ayia Marina and Portes.

This same road continues alongside the pretty villages, finally ending up at Ayia Marina, which we discussed in the previous route.

Marathon
Perdika

*T*he route taken to reach Perdika is idyllic and peaceful, not at all like the others we have covered so far. The road, which follows the coast with almost no bends at all, proceeds alongside the neo-classical villas near to the port of Faros. From here on, it continues alongside the coast of the gulf of Marathon.

This is the open gulf in which the Greek war ships gathered after their victory at Salamis in order to divide the spoils. It is also the gulf at which Capodistrias, the first governor of Greece after the Revolution of 1821, disembarked in order to set up his first government.

The village of **Marathon** appears after a total of 4 kilometres from the port of Aegina. Marathon has an organised beach and has developed into a tourist resort. From here on, the houses become fewer and fewer. There is a small strip of land in between the road and the coast, which has a fair covering of greenery. Eucalyptus trees, with their tall and slender trunks, bushes, reeds, and behind all this lies the sea, peaceful, alight, with an amazing blue colour, the shades of which fluctuate as the distance from the coast increases.

Further in the distance, on a bare, long and narrow peninsula, the white houses of Perdika shine in the light of the sun. Moni, the conical-shaped islet, stands out to the right, and behind all this, the sharp dark grey-blue peaks of the Methana mountain range.

A little before Perdika, the organised beach of Aiginitissa, with its beautiful sands and green surroundings, most definitely attracts the visitor's eye.

At this point the road ascends, now entering the infertile earth of Perdika. Yet, even in this treeless place, which is watered on both sides by the sea, a surprise awaits the visitor. On the southern side of the peninsula there is a charming fishing village which, despite its tourist development, has managed to preserve all the features of the Aegean Sea which charac-terised it of old. Its port, full of colourful fishing caiques and other boats, buzzes with life.

The raised road above the port, with the tavernas all in a row on one side and the little tables set up along the seafront on the other, remains just as it was many years ago. A few small hotels and rented rooms have, of course, now been added. The place has been noticeably developed, the large church of Ayios Sozos, which celebrates its feast day on 7 September with a large festival in the village, built. Yet, the village's charm is still the same.

1. The village and beach at Marathon.
2. The beach at Aeginitissa.

The visitor coming from the town of Aegina (9 km. away) will enjoy walking through the village lanes, with their old houses and gardens full of flowers, as well as trying some fresh fish - something never absent from Perdika.

The visitor can even, if it is the right season, visit the islet of **Moni** opposite, and enjoy a -wonderful swim in its fantastically - clean waters. It is only a short distance away, and there are regular connections throughout the summer months.

You disembark at a small, organised sandy beach on a cove on the north coast of the islet. A beautiful forest stretches out beyond the beach, clambering up the slope of a steep mountain and covering almost the whole of the northern area of Moni. The rest of the islet is bare and craggy, with rocks at its highest point, which tapers off into a cone. The island belongs to the Greek Travellers' Club, and rare species of animals are nurtured on it, such as the chamois Cretan goat-antelope and peacocks.

From Perdika, a relatively new road leading to the east goes to the village of Sfentouri, on the north slope of Mt Oros (Profitis Ilias).

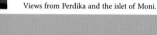

Views from Perdika and the islet of Moni.

Angistri

Skala, with the brilliant-white church of the Ayii Anargyri.

*F*rom the port of Aegina, it appears like a dark-green stroke of paint over the blue sea of the Saronic Gulf. The little island of Angistri is so full of pine trees that in antiquity it was called Pityousa, from pitys, a pine-bearing tree today known as koukounaria ('pine cone'). The ancients also called the island Kekryfaleia, a name mentioned by Homer, who tells us that during the Trojan War it was allied with Aegina. The archaeological finds from the island indicate that it was inhabited by at least 500 BC.

Angistri lies around 3.5 nautical miles to the west of Aegina, and 22 nautical miles south-west of Piraeus. It has an area of 13 square kilometres, the largest part of which is covered in pine forests, olive groves, almond and fig trees.

The ferryboats coming from Aegina and Piraeus moor at **Skala**, the natural harbour on the north-east coast of the island. This is also where most people come, and there are many hotels and tavernas to serve the needs of visitors.

Views from Skala, the harbour of Angistri.

The beach at Halkiada.

The large, brilliant-white church of the Ayii Anargyri, which dominates the port and is visible from quite a distance away, is impressive. The church celebrates its feast day on 1 July, when there is a great fair. Above Skala, on the slopes of the mountain, is the village of **Metochi**, with a panoramic view over the beach and the sea. A coastal road leading from Skala in a south-westerly direction, passes first by the beach of **Skliri** and terminates at the pebbly beach of **Halkiada**.

Again from Skala, the central coastal road in the opposite direction (to the west) leads after 2 kilometres to **Mylos**, or, as it was later named, **Megalochori** (Big Village). This is the island's largest village and also its capital. There is a harbour here at which the small boats which service local connections mainly moor (there is a marina), and there is also a pebbly beach for swimming.

Megalochori and Skala share between them the island's hotels, rented rooms and tavernas. The metropolitan church of Megalochori is the Zoodochos Pigi, which celebrates its feast day on Easter Sunday.

From the raised area above the harbour of Megalochori, which is on the north edge of the island, the road turns now towards the south, following the coast but this time from above and at a distance from the coast. Within the thick forests, the beautiful bays with the azure waters begin to make their appearance. One of these is the lovely beach of **Dragonara**, which can be reached via a little turning to the right.

After a total of five kilometres from Mylos, the road terminates at **Limenaria**, the island's fourth village. Here, there is a handful of tavernas and the church of Ayia Kyriaki, which celebrates its feast day on 7 July, when there is a great fair. The route from Metochi to Skala, Mylos and Limenaria is serviced by a local bus. Turning once more, this time in a westerly direction, the road from Limenaria

leads to a strange landscape with a singular beauty. Before reaching the coast, the road passes a small harbour and finally terminates at the sea, opposite the islet of Aponiso which lies next to Angistri. Further beyond is the larger islet of Dorousa which, along with the area's other sights, creates a picture of exceptional splendour.

Angistri, with its beautiful, primitive nature, good tourism facilities, the water sports and nightlife it has to offer the young, and, foremost, its beautiful, clean beaches, is a most attractive option which will continue to attract an ever-increasing number of visitors.

Views from Angistri.

Salamis is the second largest of the Saronic islands and the nearest to Athens. It is covered in pine trees and has beautiful beaches, especially on the south coast. The island is best known for the historic Battle of Salamis, which took place in 480 BC between the victorious Athenians and the Persians.

Salamis

Hydra is a wonderful, cosmopolitan society unto itself. With its rich history, the island stands out for its charm and the grand mansions of the captains and notables of the 1821 War of Independence. Cars are forbidden on Hydra, and transport to the beaches is by caique only.

Hydra

ᴐᴜND AEGINA

Spetses lies at the entrance to the Saronic Gulf. It is the island of Bouboulina, the heroine of the Greek revolution. The many pine trees are a characteristic feature of the island, which in antiquity was known as Pityousa (pitys, yos = pine). There are also charming horse-drawn carriages, beautiful beaches and grand mansions.

Spetses

Poros

Poros means passage, and this is where the name of the island comes from, since it lies in the south-east of the Saronic Gulf, opposite the Argolid in the Peloponnese. Located on the edge of this passage, built on both sides of a hill, this island society is a happy one.

USEFUL INFORMATION

For Aegina, Angistri,take the boat or ferry from Piraeus (information: Piraeus Port Authority tel. 210 4593123). For a quicker journey, you can take the speedboat, again from Piraeus (from Akti Miaoulis or Zea). Information: Minoan Flying Dolphins, tel. 210 4199200. In addition to its main port, Aegina also has two other ports, Souvala and Ayia Marina, to which you can go directly from Piraeus by boat or speedboat, whilst you can also go to Angistri from Aegina with small boats (in the summer). There are daily connections for all these journeys, with more daily connections in the summer and less in the winter.

There are many hotels and rented rooms in Aegina, both in the town and in the other areas. Local buses run throughout the whole island.

USEFUL TELEPHONE NUMBERS

AEGINA **22970**	Municipality 22220	Municipal
Health Centre 22222	Taxis 22635	District 61073
Police 23333	**AYIA MARINA** **22970**	**ANGISTRI** **22970**
Tourist	Rural Doctor's Surgery 32175	Rural Doctor's Surgery 91251
Police 27777	Port Authority 32358	Police 91201
Port Authority 22328	**PERDIKA** **22970**	Community Offices . . . 91260

HOTELS

AEGINA (22970)

AEGINITIKO	ISIDORAS . . . . C ..32414	VAGIA . . . . E ..71179
ARCHONTIKO . . . . . . .A ..24968	CAROUSEL . . . . C ..32496	**Perdika**
DANAI . . . . B ..22424	KARAS . . . . C ..32464	ILIOPERATO . . . . C ..61455
MIRANDA . . . . B ..22266	CARYATIDES . . . . C ..32331	SISSY (**Marathon**) . . . .D ..26222
MICHAIL MARA . . . . B ..26421	CLEOPATRA . . . . C ..32038	MOODY BAY
NAUSICA . . . . B ..22333	KYRIAKAKIS . . . . C ..32588	(**Profitis Ilias**) . . . . B ..61166
AEGINA . . . . C ..22472	LIBERTY . . . . C ..32353	**Souvala**
ARETI . . . . C ..23593	LIBERTY II ' . . . . C ..32645	EFI . . . . C ..52214
AVRA . . . . C ..22303	MAGDA . . . . C ..32325	SARONIKOS . . . . D ..52224
KLONOS . . . . C ..25874	BLUE SUNDRIVE . . . . C ..32646	
NERINA . . . . C ..23038	BLUE HORIZON . . . . . C ..32303	**ANGISTRI (22970)**
PAVLOU . . . . C ..22795	NEKTARIOS . . . . C ..32438	**Megalochori**
ATHENA PAVLOU . . . D ..23011	OASIS . . . . C ..32312	MYLOS . . . . .D ..91241
ARTEMIS . . . . D ..25195	AGONES . . . . C ..32110	AKTI . . . . E ..91232
MARMARINOS . . . . . .D ..23510	PANORAMA . . . . C ..32202	NONDAS . . . . E ..91209
PEPPAS . . . . .D ..23793	PANTELAROS . . . . C ..32431	FLOISVOS . . . . E ..91264
ULRIKA . . . . E ..25600	PICCADILY . . . . C ..32646	
TOYAH . . . . E ..24242	POSEIDONN . . . . C ..32392	ANDREAS . . . . .D ..91346
CHRISTINA . . . . E ..25600	SANDY BEACH . . . . . . C ..32149	GALINI . . . . .D ..91530
Ayia Marina	TA TRIA ADELFIA . . . C ..32229	MANARAS . . . . D ..91312
APOLLO . . . . B ..32271	VILLA MARIOLIS . . . .D ..32495	SARONIS . . . . .D ..91394
ARGO . . . . B ..32266	CAVOS . . . . .D ..32338	ANGISTRI . . . . E ..91288
KATERINA . . . . B ..32205	ALEXANDROS . . . . E ..32365	AKTAION . . . . E ..91222
AIGLI . . . . C ..32221	ANTHI . . . . E ..32565	ALEXANDRA . . . . E ..91251
AKTI . . . . C ..32249	ANGELA . . . . E ..32556	ANAGENESIS . . . . E ..91332
AMOUDIA . . . . C ..32213	DELPHINI . . . . E ..32451	ANASTASIOU . . . . E ..91317
APHAIA . . . . C ..32227	BAKOMITROA . . . . E ..32442	ARTEMIS . . . . E ..91309
GALANI . . . . C ..32203	MYRMIDON . . . . E ..32646	YIANNA . . . . E ..91228
ERATO . . . . C ..32592	RAUMA . . . . E ..32168	MARY . . . . E ..91421
HERMES . . . . C ..32411	**Vaia**	PAGONA . . . . E ..91122
	XENI . . . . C ..71150	POULAKIS . . . . E ..91353

Note: The dialling system has been changed and the area code is now prefixed to each number for all calls.

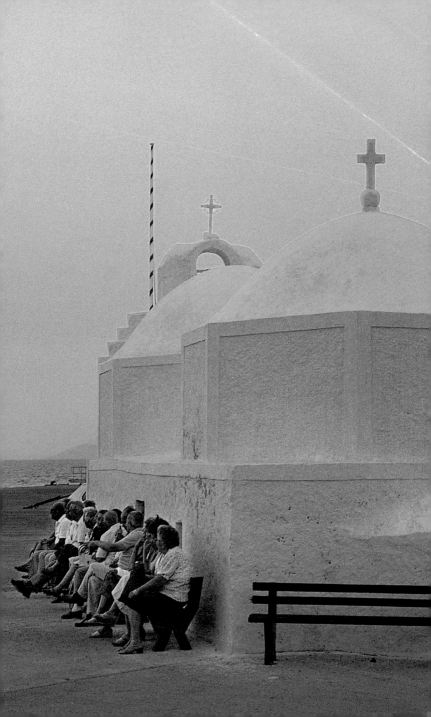

INDEX

Text: GIANNIS DESYPRIS
Coordination: DAPHNE CHRISTOU
Translation: DESPINA CHRISTODOULOU
Artistic editor: EVI DAMIRI

Production - Printing: M. Toubis S.A..